The Plummer Bible

by

D. Brian Plummer

published by

TIDELINE
Publications Promotions

published by
Tideline Publications Promotions

49 KINMEL STREET, RHYL, DENBIGHSHIRE,
NORTH WALES LL18 1AG
TEL: 01745 354919 ext 52 or 07939 877175
FAX: 01745 356919

printed by Gwasg Helygain Ltd
68-70 Kinmel Street, Rhyl LL18 1AW
Tel 01745 331411   Fax 01745 331310
info@gwasg.com   www.gwasg.com

ISBN 978 0 9552179 4 4

INTRODUCTION
By Sue Rothwell

The Plummer Bible
Written by D. Brian Plummer

Within the pages of this document, you will read about the creation of the Plummer Terrier and how Brian saw a vision for his dogs and their future. His aim was to encourage enthusiasts to take these dogs forward with the possibility of eventually creating a new breed of dogs which would and could be instantly recognised.

Written in the late 1980s, and with only a handful of dogs in existence, the Plummer Bible was a 'guide' to assist potential breeders in choosing suitable stock in order to maximise the potential of breeding due to the restricted gene pool. You will note that 'Non Pure' dogs are mentioned, yet, still considered desirable for use as 'Outcross blood' being introduced into the then 'melting pot'. This historical 'document' explains, breeding and troubleshooting in laymens terms for both the novice and experienced breeder, or more importantly enthusiasts of the breed. The Plummer Bible enforces and cements our beliefs that the term 'pure' cannot and should not be applied to any of these dogs – yet!!

Brian does contradict himself within these pages as to what he saw as the future for the dogs, by not taking into account the possible occurrence of the sexual dimorphism gene which manifested itself within the breed in the mid to late 1990s, due to the then restrictive gene pool. In an attempt to bring these dogs back into line he saw no alternative but to re-introduce bull terrier blood back into the gene pool in order to break it. This was done in 1998, amidst much controversy which is still present today.

The formation of The Plummer Terrier Club of Great Britain by Brian before his untimely death, secured a future for the breed as a whole, gave people choices which is what he wanted. Thankfully, before Brian passed away he left a blueprint for the future of the breed taking into account possible re-occurrence of old and any new problems we may encounter.

Let's hope we can do him justice over the coming years by continuing his work and securing a future for the terrier which carries his name – *The Plummer Terrier*.

THE PLUMMER
TERRIER BIBLE

The future of the line:

I shall mate the Salem x Kotian bitch. I call her Barad – Hebrew for "fear or dread", to Jerry Boyle's Hector to produce a suitable bitch line for you. Hector is a truly beautiful animal and free of the faults Barad is likely to breed.

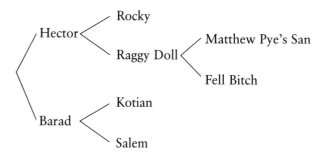

I'm going to lend Salem to Jed or get her mated to Hector and put out bitches to you and Jed and possibly Bill Mossman.

A buyer from Pontefract is going to contact you for a bitch puppy to set up a Kennel to breed working terriers. He is unlikely to do you any harm, for you will have a good name by the time he gets big enough to be a rival. Teach him about how to keep a line 'tight'. At this stage you must allow public use of studs for at least five years.

You are liable to use Rocky far too much and you need younger slightly related stud dogs. You will need a pure bred, properly marked son or grandson of Rupert and a son of Matthew's dog San. You must breed them fairly quickly as you will institute a load of problems if you do not because:

a) Rocky bred bitches will be brought back and you will have nothing to mate to them.
b) People will either inbreed to the wrong males if you do not.
c) People will outcross if you can't provide good stud dogs.
d) A state of chaos will prevail and you can't afford this to happen at this stage in the breed development.

When you put dogs to stud observe the following rules:

a) Explain to buyers that the fee is for the mating not only when conception occurs.
b) Explain fee is to be paid before the bitch leaves the premises.
c) Stud pedigree copy only when the fee is paid.
d) Request photographs of the puppies bred.
e) Insist tails are docked properly.
f) Insist your ways are observed to the letter.
g) Never take a puppy in lieu of fee – in nine cases out of ten you won't get the puppy.
h) Start collecting working certificates and display

them around your kennels.

i)   Breed duplicate studs: i.e. Pazzaz and Phobos, and put one or both to hunt service until they are ready to breed.

Don't ever try to get bogus work certificates as you are only fooling yourself by doing this and always give free return matings if the bitch 'misses'. Get a reputation for being totally honest and fair in all things. When you make enemies, and as you become more successful you will, honesty will be your only defence. In all it matters keep your integrity – your move regarding replacing Jed's puppy was a good one. In many ways you must have been educated to the ways of terrier buyers by now. If you have the slightest doubt about potential buyers don't sell them puppies. Even if you miss a sale you'll eventually sell the puppy to a suitable buyer. Remember every 'suitable' buyer is an advertisement. Don't ever allow a 'bidder' to buy a puppy – the 'bidder' is always an unsatisfactory client. Even if the 'bidder' eventually comes up with the money you ask, don't sell to him – he's had practise at under bidding others before he came to you. Avoid selling to people of this ilk. Avoid having trash of this sort to your kennels – and he'll have like friends aplenty. Don't encourage meddlers or dealers. Someone who is doing the rounds of the kennels will bring some disease to your kennels. Keep people like this at bay, but sooner or later you will need to inject against parvo virus and add the price on to your puppies. Many of your buyers will have had this breed before and will be prepared to pay the price you ask.

In fact, in the next year or so you will be selling quite a few puppies to people who have worked the breed before.

Treat people who claim to have owned lots of terriers with care as they will get you a bad name, as nothing they buy will ever be any good.

Don't ever deal in part-started dogs. The sort of people who will take on an adult or sapling dog are a bad bet anyway. However a quick and easy way of making money is to take cat killers, bad stock worriers put them to hunt service, sell them and give a working certificate in with the purchase. Such a dog is worth at least £300 and never accept less!

Nearly every puppy you produce has the potential to be a bad cat killer and cat killers will usually kill or at least 'work' foxes. Don't give such dogs 'on trial'. It takes a full year to enter a cat killer at hunt service and it only takes an hour to ruin the dog. If you sell a trained dog, sell a working certificate with it – a working certificate is worth more than a trial. Never take back damaged dogs or dogs that quit cold – it takes a year to get the terriers 'confident' again and a year in kennels is worth far more than £300. This is a good rule to observe and £300 is very little to ask for a trained dog.

Supply the hunt you frequent with any coloured F1 you may get returned and let the huntsman use the terrier for a full season before you sell the dog. This transaction will cost you nothing and gets you a good name for terriers – though I don't like the sale of grown dogs of any breed. People who can't start dogs are usually quite good at ruining dogs.

The 'Kiss of Death' for a serious breeder is the sale of 'just ready' dogs or 'nearly trained saplings'. People who are prepared to buy such dogs are meddlers who will not allow a sapling to settle before expecting it to enter on the first outing. These are the buyers who will ruin your name. Avoid the one who wants a dog 'just ready to start' like the plague – these are really the 'red light signs' of the terrier world and may well use up to ten or twelve 'just ready' dogs a year. Few of these people will ever get satisfactory dogs from anyone. Expressions like 'have you got a dog doing a bit' set my teeth on edge – and they will eventually antagonise you.

Buy a Collins desk diary and write it up each day.

The importance of honesty and integrity cannot be overstressed.

To return to the stud dogs – you will need more than you imagine and, more to the point you will need a variety of studs.

To continue the line you or Bill or Jed will need a Matthew bred stud San x perhaps a Rocky bred bitch.

A Rupert stud (you have one) but Jed should breed

another.

A Rocky son – a first rate animal – the best he can breed.

Bear in mind stud dogs will need to be available for incoming bitches – and in three years you will get a lot of stud bitches.

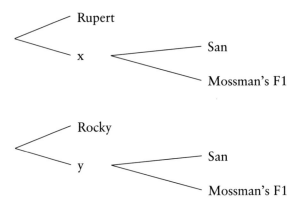

Anyway if they pass one to you it will ease the inbreeding that seems inevitable. If need be I will breed a San bred bitch.

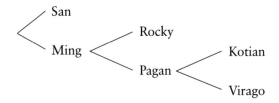

The Plummer Bible

This will provide a San bred stud without the hepatid patella problem you bred from Firebird to San.

This is probably the most important document you will ever have in your collection, so keep it safe.

Two factors come into play at this time 22nd October 1990.

Matthew's dog is old and you will be forced to inbreed to Rocky, this is not altogether good as:

- Rocky is a chance mix up
- Rocky has a low IQ
- He throws putty noses
- If he dies you are in a mess

You will need a stud that is only slightly related. Chalcroft's dog is ideal except for:

- Distance
- He is Rocky's son
- He carries black and white
- He also carries rough coat, which is not important under the circumstances, as we will not inbreed to him

Two new studs should be bred. I shall continue from one – you from another.

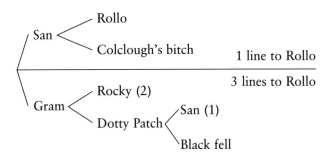

San
Rollo
Colclough's bitch

1 line to Rollo

3 lines to Rollo

Gram
Rocky (2)
Dotty Patch
San (1)
Black fell

This dog + dog (yours and mine) are 1/3 bred to Rollo. An even more ideal breeding might be:

¼ Rollo

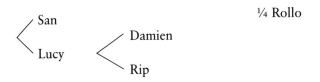

San
Lucy
Damien
Rip

An alternative would be:

¼ Rollo

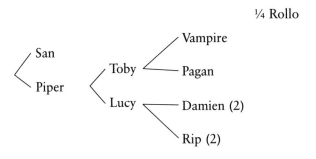

San
Piper
Toby
Vampire
Pagan
Lucy
Damien (2)
Rip (2)

Either cross will provide a suitable stud. Lucy might be better, but she will bite through a wall.

If one of these is bought or bred then (a) you have breathing space to inbreed to Rocky.

PLAN 1

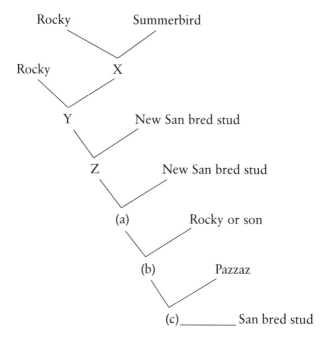

Rocky   Summerbird

Rocky   X

Y   New San bred stud

Z   New San bred stud

(a)   Rocky or son

(b)   Pazzaz

(c)_____ San bred stud

By this time you will be going it alone without help or guidance from me – I feel you may be forced for obvious reasons. Don't bring tiny heads in except for every four or five generations (Pazzaz and Phobos) and don't keep males from them. Interchange blood with Colclough (Piper or his ½ bred bitch) both to San. You will need several San bred dogs on tap. One with me and one with Mossman – swop him a Gram x San male or even a Rocky daughter.

Kotian's death was a tragedy but not the end of the world. I can and will breed you one better. Sell all San bred males to serious breeders – note where they go. I will if I am able send you two bitches bred thus:

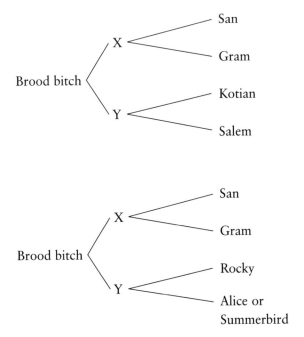

You will need to place males from Matthew Pye's dog with non-swoppers. San should be used regularly or your line will die out.

Don't forget Dotty Patch carries this factor and so do her daughters – encourage people to inbreed to San – via coloured bitches. Weave in a few Rupert outcrosses while you can – if what you say is correct, you may not have time to do this. A good terrier man knows when to retire a dog.

Keep a desk diary (the £7 Boots or Woolworths variety) and fill it every day – don't leave gaps. This is the most important time in the history of the breed so copy down pedigrees and further irregularities in the breeding.

WIDEN THE GENE POOL

If your chocolate bitch breeds good stuff to Rocky mate her or another puppy from her, to Rupert. Pollit bred two litters from Damien. Check where most of them went. Rocky, Rupert, Lucy?

If the idiot fraternity are prepared to breed from Lucy or her puppies then by all means buy a puppy. The trouble is they mess about and kennel everything together – with ugly results. Your first priority is therefore: To breed two dogs:

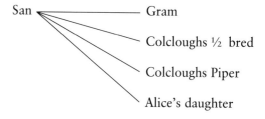

San
— Gram
— Colcloughs ½ bred
— Colcloughs Piper
— Alice's daughter

You must never <u>inbreed</u> to Matthew's dog i.e San x daughter, San x granddaughter is possibly fine. Don't inbreed to a son of San either.

Ideally there should be two stud dogs from San. a) San x Piper and / or b) San x Gram and / or c) San x Mossman's ½ bred (Pip x Teen). You must keep one preferably from a) or c) and I must keep a ½ brother. Periodically we must change stud dogs to facilitate Plan 1.

In some five years time there will be plenty of sundry stud dogs available, but if you don't get studs from Matthew, you cannot continue the line at all. If you continue to use Matthew's dog all will be good, <u>but you don't want a puppy from the</u> Sailor x ½ bred bitch. By the time I have, you must have at least 40 males and 250 bitches to get a big enough gene pool. Encourage Bachner to breed at least 2 stud dogs and build up your sales by frequent articles and reference to Plummer terriers. Every good bitch must be sold as a brood. Take care not to inbreed too closely to <u>Kotian</u> – you will throw a Russell coloured puppy at times. Rocky* will breed bad markings if you inbreed to him. Rupert <u>must</u> be marked, he can't be otherwise so you are wrong!

TRY NOT TO BREED IN THIS PATCH.

Settle on breeding a larger headed Phobos or Pazzaz.

Continue to pump out puppies from Firebird x Matthew's San. Breed every season. Keep best bitches and keep records of all places where males are sold. Above all encourage <u>all</u> clients to breed from their bitches to pure bred males. I shall try to increase your lines via different ways.

Toby may be a superb dog to use on bitches,

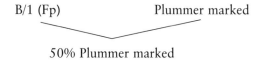

B/1 (Fp)   Plummer marked

50% Plummer marked

Toby is the last survivor of the first F2 hybrid crop – you might do well to consider him – he is a top grade badger finder and the best stayer around – a very legend of a dog, but not a fast dog.

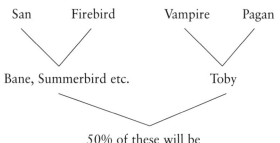

San   Firebird   Vampire   Pagan

Bane, Summerbird etc.   Toby

50% of these will be
Plummer marked:- could be a stud dog

This would give not only breathing space but keep good heads while you seek to counterbalance with

Rupert / Rocky lines. The line also nearly replicates genes of San and may be the ideal alternative line to use if San dies before you have your pack established. Also Kotian or Phobos / Deimos / Pazzaz would be an ideal classy outcross for this line. Do not begrudge the 50% coloured crop (fell type) you will breed from Toby – you must accept loss of marking to get the very best workers, even the coloured puppies will be saleable once you've made a name for yourself. Get as many colour photographs of properly marked stock as you can. I've given your name to Ian Johnson – get him to do colour photographs for the front of "Shooting News". Send the photograph of Toby back to me – and keep the list of available stock.

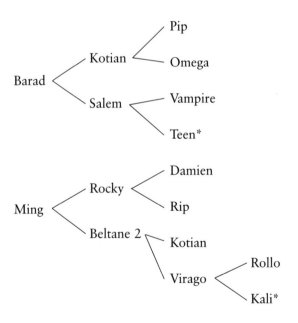

If you inbreed to Beltane* then the chance of 'raised' or 'pricked' ears increases. Hence studs 'today' (current studs) which carry Beltane's blood should be bred from Matthew's stud to produce houndy ears. Don't underestimate the value of Matthew's stud, and use him all you can. Your studs should be bred from him or from his houndy eared children.

Try to breed away from Virago – though her children are wonderfully game and have excellent noses.

If you double up on Rocky's progeny watch for ears in the progeny – they need to have some of San's blood in the next generation if you are to keep the ears down.

Patella troubles were brought in by a dog called Laddie.

Warlock
Vampire
Beltane

Laddie

Jennie

Hulmer, his dogs or bitches manifested this peculiarity but Omega carried and passed it on via Kotian and Rollo. However it appears most frequently when Rollo and Kotian lines are close in the pedigrees.

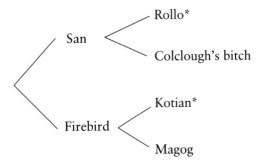

This explains the luxated patella.

The studs available at time of writing are:

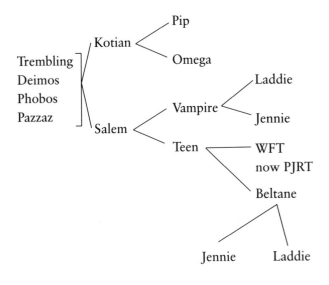

The Plummer Bible

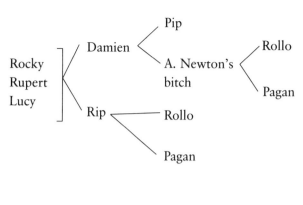

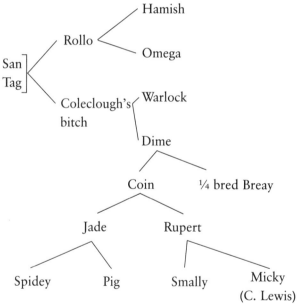

(Tagisstenle)

Basically only <u>three</u> radically different studs exist and it is therefore imperative that more and better studs are bred. At the time or writing Curtis is leaning too heavily on Rocky – he has agreed to favour San in 1991. Both Bill and you should also get as many puppies from him as you can – particularly to Rocky bred bitches, San should be used extensively as a) he breeds bad coats and the line lack substance. If Curtis breeds a top grade male from San x Lucy then use it as often as is feasible – even half brother, half sister breedings if the San x Lucy male is top rate. If anything happens to me before 1995 try to remember – don't double up on the line from Magog.

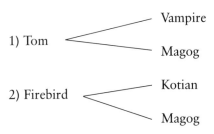

1) Tom — Vampire
— Magog

2) Firebird — Kotian
— Magog

The dam of Magog has a terrible mouth effect – only the carnassial teeth come through in the permanent mouth – and even the carnissial teeth had no proper roots. However the offspring were the most game dogs and bitches I have ever bred. Don't double up on the line however and always check pedigrees before mating. If Magog is close up in a dog or bitches pedigree don't mate to a dog or bitch with the same type of pedigree.

If I had the time – and I am aware I haven't, it would

be expedient to bring in new blood via Muriel's stock if it is typey enough – the nervousness of Muriel's animal is due to lack of a socialising programme and is not innate. If there is time – and Sam is old and has a heart illness (I know the feeling) then a stud from Muriel's puppy and San would be useful. The true breeding nature of the type is indicated by the fact that even after several generations of Russell outcrosses the type appears in Muriel's litters from time to time. It is also worth noting that the white triangle that appeared in Rocky's litter came off the family before Pollit meddled with the patterns. Muriel's line is bred thus: (before the constant matings to JRT)

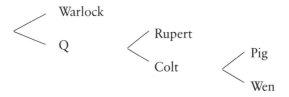

Warlock

Q

Rupert

Colt

Pig

Wen

Thus Muriel's line may be useful and it might be worth breeding from her best animals. However, she gave Curtis a very wild dog and I believe he put it out to a pet home as it refused to come to hand. Still it might be reasonable to include some of Muriel's stock in the gene pool if;

a)   Colour, working instinct and nose do not suffer.

b)   Type is maintained – straight legs, elegance and the length of leg is consistent.

Nevertheless studs should <u>not </u>be taken from Muriel's stock – though half breds may be ideal for continuing the line. Anyway Muriel should be encouraged to breed from her puppy, most certainly Q had the best nose the line has produced since the beagle outcross – she was also part bull terrier blood so the line is well worth thinking about.

It is therefore policy to find serious breeders as 'stolons' – although the process smacks of evangelising. However, no one should consider selling a top rate bitch without giving the buyer advice on the future breeding of the line. It may also be policy to draw up a list of suitable stud dogs and the addresses of their owners.

It is bad policy to introduce mavericks, meddlers and dealers into the ranks of breeders and mavericks are more dangerous than dealers. Don't allow registration of some dogs that resemble the pure lines but cannot produce proof of ancestors that date to that line. For instance some breeders have offered the heavily marked Russells as Plummers. Stop this before it starts and once the craze for breeding the type stalls and it will, there will be many quasi breeders creeping out of the woodwork with heavily patched dogs seeking registration. Hence a register, and an accurate one to be started.

Muriel's puppy should be used wisely and with great care. Try a litter and watch a) type, b) performance, c) courage of the progeny before breeding another. If your prices are kept high (and you must ignore "I want a really good puppy, but I don't want to pay much" and put them into the bin) then you will need to select buyers – particularly to the Muriel lines. Sales wise the following graph is certain to be appropriate.

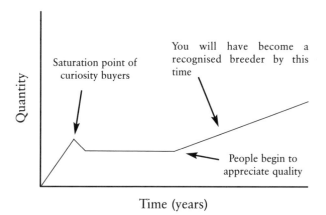

Time (years)

You will eventually be able to sell approximately 300 puppies a year – but never any more unless you "cash in" on America and Australia. I've never been a salesman or organiser. You will need to advertise to make a name for yourself, but above all you will need absolute honesty and integrity to succeed. Honesty to the letter must always be the order of the day.

In the next month or so I shall send you a data card with advice on entering and rearing a puppy. Photocopy it and give a copy to the breeder / customer. If advice is heeded all these puppies will go and go well.

As you progress and start to flourish you will also need to give a stud card with <u>bitch</u> puppies listing the stud dogs you have to encourage the buyer to bring back the bitch for mating. I wish to do this for you. The cost of producing these cards will be met by ½ the stud fee for the first mating and will bring you in a lot of stud fees.

Learn to deal with meddlers quickly and politely if you can, but don't hesitate to offend a 'macho' man. Try: Does your psychiatrist know you are out?; You are clearly in need of medical treatment or more stingingly; I want my dogs to go to good homes; You are boring me now, Good night; Simply put the phone down when the idiot is in full flight. Simply state "I don't want to sell you a puppy". Don't get into arguments – and after you've delivered the punch line replace the receiver immediately. Cultivate the image of integrity and always refund the money whatever the cause of the complaint. Don't replace puppies. Get an idiot to buy elsewhere. Don't ever offer to swop puppies and stay away from trading in grown dogs and crossbreds. Charge a stud fee – you can easily buy a puppy and you will seldom get a puppy in lieu of fee anyway. Give return matings free if the bitch fails to conceive.

Make all documents authentic <u>and</u> attractive. People enjoy having attractive documentation with their puppies. i.e. pedigree, advice sheet and stud list.

A stud list is important, it costs roughly £30 per year

to keep a stud dog – and it will easily pay for its keep once you are established. Your documentation should therefore be professionally produced and should look good. When you have enough stud dogs run advertisements in the sporting press advertising them.

Never haggle over price even if you have surplus puppies that are difficult to sell. Never haggle over refunding on an inoculated dog anyway. When a lunatic brings dogs back, take it back, refund wholly and put the dog to hunt service <u>but</u> tell your huntsman what has happened. Avoid dishonesty at all costs. When I shuffle off these mortal coils, I don't want to come back from the shades to find you have become a meddler. Integrity and honest breeding is the only way to success.

Estimate a bitch will breed eight puppies every two litters or 8/1 x 2/15 = 6.6/15 per annum or £600 per bitch – always calculate on the low side and then you can afford to be disappointed.

£600 per year = £500 profit

£500 per bitch = 20 bitches to live at £10,000 per year.

Stud fees cannot be calculated, but bear in mind:

Sales competition
from others

Stud fees

The logic of selling half-trained dogs escapes most 'dodos'. If an unsold puppy is 'run on' to be sold, or with the expressed purpose of being sold, it is clearly a poor structured dog – it is obviously the last puppy in the litter to be sold and hence probably, though not always, the poorest puppy in the litter. It therefore follows that 'a just starting puppy' is fairly certainly sub-standard as it was not sold 'straight from the nest'. To price a trained or ready for starting puppy or sapling assume; £100 (initial price) - £10 (it is the worst puppy) = £90. Inoculation (it is madness to run on an uninoculated puppy) = £30. It costs roughly £1 a week to keep a terrier (and that doesn't include your time rearing, feeding and training). If a puppy or sapling is sold at 10 months of age this requires an extra 32 weeks of 'keep' from when the puppy was weaned at 8 weeks old. At £1 a week, this is £32. Therefore the puppy is worth (£100 - £10) = £90 + £30 inoculation + £32 = £152.

However, this does not take into account the cost of kennelling and basic training – how much is turning over galvanised sheets to catch mice worth or several sessions of ratting? So the cost of an unentered puppy

= £152 + whatever price you wish to put on your time. At the barest minimum you are asking for £250 for an untrained or partly trained puppy.

It might pay you to offer grown trained dogs at £500 + (or from £500) in your next advert. This will put off the lunatic element, though it will invite them at first. It will however put off the fool seeking 'a dog doing a bit' or 'just ready for starting'. It may also make people realise how much it costs to train a terrier.

I wouldn't sell any more top grade bitches from Alice – and Chalcroft will carry Parvo virus until next Christmas by the way – so don't let him near your puppies. (Alice x Rocky) x (San x Lucy) would keep you going until 2000 AD. A point to remember is that two brothers have different genes.

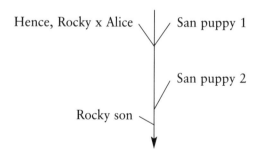

Hence, Rocky x Alice   San puppy 1

                             San puppy 2

Rocky son

A line is quite easy to continue if you adopt this three, stud system – though it is easier if the studs are only slightly related. A 'shift around' of studs will help.

I will buy a stud and lend it to you for a season and hence to other members of the circle. If they are prepared to do the same with you – the problem of keeping too many males is solved – but it means that all of us must keep together. In the next few months I shall take a line of Trembling's sister Barad, I shall mate her to Rupert or San and mate Rocky to the progeny and continue a line in Caithness. I can then set in motion a line that will provide an income for Norma if things go wrong with me. It would be useful if you would sell top class stock for Norma. Abstract any top rate bitches for yourself, but watch for peculiar hindquarters in any puppies from Kotian x Salem bloodlines. If I can I will put together a pack of perhaps twenty bitches – and they will be top flight stock. I have a mating that may produce a litter.

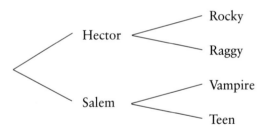

If I get good bitches I shall keep them or we'll share <u>really</u> top grade puppies, I have a few quite grotty bitches Kotian x Virago that will breed good stuff if mated to Rocky – or rather good stuff, for if you lean too heavily on Kotian / Rocky bloodlines you will get pale putty nosed bitches. If you pull off the Bachner and Lucy projects you will not need to use Russell or Fell outcrosses, and you will eventually breed out putty noses. It can be done so try and absorb this formula. If you keep back a putty nose bitch – or get someone else to keep one - then the putty nose is recessive to normal dark nosed stock. Hence if a dog is able to throw a putty nosed puppy if mated to a putty nosed bitch the dog too must carry putty nosed genes.

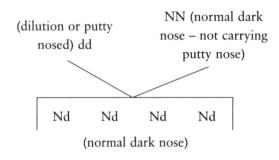

(dilution or putty nosed) dd

NN (normal dark nose – not carrying putty nose)

| Nd | Nd | Nd | Nd |

(normal dark nose)

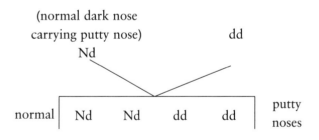

(normal dark nose carrying putty nose) Nd

dd

| normal | Nd | Nd | dd | dd | putty noses |

It's a lengthy process, but one you must attempt or tolerate putty noses in the family for many years to come. Once you breed a stud or series of studs that do not carry the factor your troubles are over. Remember the dictum 'A stud dog is half a Kennel'. Incidentally, the first sign of kennel blindness is a desire to keep back more males that <u>you</u> consider to be superior. You will need a replacement for Rocky – I would choose one of his inbred daughters: Alice, Nyad perhaps but be careful about the use of the puppy from the chocolate.

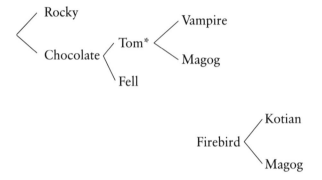

You are risking deformities of the teeth mating this dog to Firebird's puppies – but only slightly. Try one mating to test the water, so to speak, but refund money without question if a deformity appears – without integrity forget breeding these dogs.

You may find some bitches produce nothing worth keeping – I would suspect Summerbird would be one such bitch, but her puppies sold and mated to Rocky certainly will.

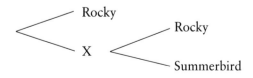

The Plummer Bible

I think incessant inbreeding to Rocky may be inevitable – he is a convenient stud, but watch for deformities if you breed too closely to him. As yet he has done nothing but good for the line, but you cannot continue to inbreed to him indefinitely.

If you produce a tan stud from (Lucy x San) there may be problems. For instance much of your income in 1994 and onwards will come from either stud fees or sale of stud puppies. People will be reluctant to use a tan stud on their bitches – no matter what you explain. Besides which only half their litter will be saleable 'Plummers'. It is a point to consider. Your studs must be typical if they are used on outside bitches. You may tolerate 50% if the 50% is top rate.

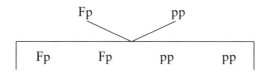

You will also need to set a bottom price limit for puppies and insist that no one under prices good puppies. You will need a set of codes of conduct to ensure this regulation is observed.

You may also wish to boycott meddlers and dealers, or those who make outcrosses without approval, once a stud register is started. I suggest that once Muriel's puppy is registered outcross blood must not be introduced. You will need perhaps ten years of methodical record keeping before you apply for KC registration but by that time you will be ready for recognition.

Maintain scrupulous honesty at all times – and throw out dishonest or questionable breeders. Pass a regulation that if a puppy falls into the hands of a dealer or meddler and its papers are lost, no new papers can be reissued. This will slow up but not stop the swopping process – and I'm afraid that until KC recognition, swopping will be the greatest curse of the breed. So far only one pure bred is known to have 'done the rounds' – though two F1's have been swopped several times. Don't allow swoppers second puppies – though it will be very difficult to stop meddlers.

Keep these papers – they will be important in the future.

PROBLEMS OF INBREEDING IN THE LINE

All sires and dams of every breed, not just ours, carry peculiarities. To minimise these problems and they need to be bred out, keep a record of the problems each terrier used in the creation of the type carries.

Vampire carries a very small head, despite his own huge head. If Vampire appears in the immediate pedigree of a dog never mate a bitch with a small head to it. Hence Barry's dog should be used with care. Laddie, father of Vampire – I suspect the foul mouth of this side of the family came about thus:

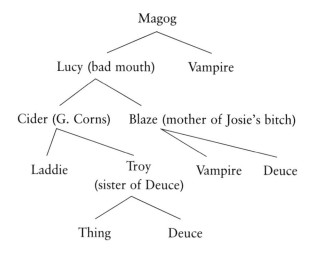

Laddie bred a puppy called Hulda from Deuce which had this foul mouth. I gave her away, and thought I had bred out the defective mouth. When Granville Corns bred the line he bred this peculiarity by unintentionally bringing the lines together – it is still in the pedigree of Mayhem bred by Di Dabinett. Barry's dog Tom, Firebird bred by Trevor Stone. Cider also carried a loose untidy coat, and this also is a pity as he was an exceedingly game dog with an outstanding nose. He would tackle badger or otter as fiercely as fox and would kill fox below and above ground. His grandchildren should not appear twice in immediate pedigrees – though there is no guarantee that any of his grandchildren carry the polygenes for the mouth, i.e.

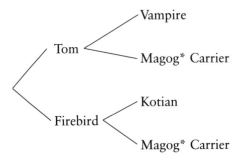

Tom
— Vampire
— Magog* Carrier

Firebird
— Kotian
— Magog* Carrier

I've bred out the influence in my own line as I've not bred from the Gog or Mayhem line. It is unwise to double up on any Gog or Maygog offspring as the bloodlines may still carry the problem. Sadly the bloodlines are very game and I've never bred an animal that looked vaguely like second rate as a worker from this line. However a line that needs watching.

Warlock, Beltane and Vampire carried chocolate colouring with putty noses if bred too closely together. Beltane bred one such puppy, but Omega didn't. It will appear if one inbreeds too closely to Vampire's line – Barry's dog carries it to certain lines – it is a polygene or so I believe.

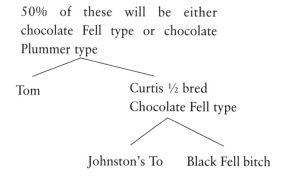

50% of these will be either chocolate Fell type or chocolate Plummer type

Tom   Curtis ½ bred Chocolate Fell type

Johnston's To   Black Fell bitch

The Rollo line is fairly safe to inbreed to – with some reservation. He produced some almost trapezoid looking offspring in bitches like Virago.

Viewed from above: Head

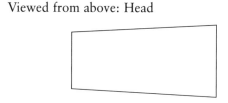

Huge heads were introduced by the Rollo's gene. Warlock had this type of head but did not breed it in his offspring.

I discontinued breeding from Warlock when he bred Patella Luxation in puppies from Warlock to his own daughter. This should be noted when breeding in Rollo genes and avoiding the popular couplings of Pagan x Rollo blood to the mix, for Pagan's grandfather was Warlock.

Whether or not Pagan carried Patella Luxation may be determined by the inbreeding programme conducted by Neil, Jeremy and Barry. Hence if Rollo blood is to be added only a limited amount must come from the Rollo x Pagan bloodlines:

Damien
Rocky
Rupert
Nipper (Toby x Lucy)
Bitch (Toby x Lucy)

Matthew's dog offers a unique chance – Rollo's blood without Pagan's.

Remember: a dog or bitch may have exactly the same genes as his litter mate or entirely different genes. If an outcross is to be made in the future it must be the best one can get, sound in instinct, sound of type and of known bloodlines. Check all lines and breed from any tested stock of good pedigree and type. The stud must be the best available blood, utterly game, with terrific nose and great instinct. An inferior untested stud is a step backwards. In future try to secure working certificates for all your males.

POSSIBILITY OF PECULIAR MOUTH "CARRYING THROUGH"

Josie's bitch was "bad mouthed" so genetically ff.

Hence Magog (Vampire x Lucy) = Gf (good, carrying foul mouth). One now has to assume none of the existing studs carry the fault so; San, Rupert, Rocky, Pazzaz, Phobos and Deimos are GG.

It also follows that good mouths are dominant to bad mouths and bad mouths recessive to good mouths. It also follows that it is impossible to determine GG from Gf. The probability factor for successive generations is as follows:

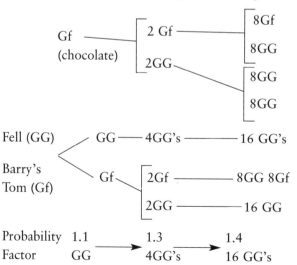

At 1.4 + it is feasible to mate to Firebird's grandchildren.

LIST OF AVAILABLE STUD DOGS AND BITCHES

<u>24 Viable Bitches</u>

Firebird – Kotian x Magog
Bitch 1 – San x Firebird
Bitch 2 – San x Firebird
Bitch 3 – San x Firebird
Alice 1 – Rocky x Virago
Alice 2 – Rocky x Virago
Handan (Jerry Boyle) – Rocky x Pagan 2
Pagan 2 – Deimos x Virago
Beltane 2 – Deimos x Virago
Dotty Patch – San x Fell
Raggy Doll – San x Fell
F2 – Deimos x Raggy Doll
F2 coloured (B. Johnson) – Deimos x Raggy
Brian (Bachner) – Rupert x (Pip x Pagan / Rollo)
F2 – Rocky x Raggy (pattern, but bad coat)
Bitch – San x Firebird
Scringe 2 – Rocky x Scringe 1
Dotty Patch 2 (Jerry Boyle) – Deimos x Raggy Doll
Tan bitch Tom Burns – Rocky x Raggy Doll
Lucy (Neil Rogers) F2 – Damien x Rip
Salem (possibly sterile) – Vampire x Teen
Virago (possibly sterile) – Rollo x Kali
Chocolate – Owd Tom x Fell
2 F2 bitches (Jem Pettit) – Owd Tom x Nipper
(Toby x Lucy)

10 Males

Kotian – Pip x Omega
Rocky – Damien x Rip
Phobos – Kotian x Salem
Deimos – Kotian x Salem
Pazzaz – Kotian x Salem
Trembling – Kotian x Salem
San – Rollo x Colclough
Rupert – Damien x Rip
Toby (Roger's) B/T – Vampire x Pagan
Owd Tom – Vampire x Magog

INTRODUCING NEW BLOOD
by Dr. D. B. Plummer

I feel this article is long overdue and if these thousand or so words 'throws the cat among the pigeons,' so be it.

Some years ago I caused a rift in the Plummer Terrier Association when I announced that I was bringing an outcross into the gene pool to improve type and possibly correct serious problems in the hindlegs of these terriers. Firstly let me explain how the terrier was created and readers may then understand why I have introduced this new blood.

In 1962 my strain of terrier was decidedly rag-tag but had a level of courage equal to any strain in the world. If they lacked anything they were a shade short on nose, hence, I introduced the blood of a small American bred Beagle. My first crosses were hideous and their pendulous ears stayed with the strain for a number of years. So did the incredible nose of the Beagle blood introduced. The new strain out hunted any type of terrier I have ever seen,and I have seen and trained, the spectrum of terrier breeds in Britain. The family also retrieved as naturally as any Springer and the wilful nature the hound blood introduced was eventually bred out. I believed then, and still do today, that I have produced the best strain of working terrier in the world and at that time my kennel housed 42 working certified dogs and bitches.

My rat pack was running well at that time and, to prevent deterioration in head size and to produce an even gamer animal, I mated some of my best bitches to a small Staffordshire Bull terrier called the Hackett white. The loss in type, colour and the increase in size in the progeny was horrifying and the progeny were sluggish and unexciting. The second generation were tigers, game as pebbles, wonderful hunters and still retained the curious retrieving instinct for which the breed is famous. This same instinct was produced in the Sporting Lucas terrier simply because 'Gwain' – a Plummer Terrier and a wonderful brood bitch was used in the creation of the Sporting Lucas. In addition to the Sporting Lucas terriers 'Pippin' and 'Coulsen's Tally', she also produced excellent Plummer Terriers. Paul Hawkes, the terrierman for the renowned Tyndale Foxhounds owns 'Billy' – a grandson of my own 'Pippin'. 'Billy' will retrieve any shot game as well as any spaniel, as would Shaun Alderton's bitch (a daughter of 'Pippin'). My ratpack was justly famous and famous sportsmen such as Ted Walsh and Frank Sheardown travelled to the midlands to watch them hunt, so did Toro Kurna of Japan, Teddy Moritz of the USA, Dr Paul Tracher of Germany – a student of Konrad Lorenz, Karl Eising of Hungary and a host of television and cinema actors and actresses. Despite the misgivings of my headmasters and my fellow lecturers it became something of an honour to be seen hunting with my pack of Plummer terriers.

Sadly, my 15 minutes of fame came to an end in 1985, June 5, to be precise, for one never forgets the date of one's first coronary. My pack was distributed among friends, became pets and were never returned to the pack when I had recovered. The Plummer Terrier Association set up to revive the breed type using a very limited gene pool for only a tiny number of terriers remained at my kennels. Hence problems were certain to arise and had I the wit or wisdom I should have re-introduced bull terrier blood to enlarge the gene pool then to prevent the inevitable problems from happening. All terriers carry undesirable qualities in their gene pools and as I write Fell terriers are very prone to Perthe's disease (degeneration of the hip joint) and Patella luxation (slipping knee cap). These problems are also rampant in Jack Russell terriers (the curious Jack Russell hopping action) and also the Plummer Terrier.

What was even more disturbing was the appearance of what is best described as a sexual dimorphism, a curious condition where males are nearly twice as heavy as the females – a peculiarity often seen in Muselids such as Ferrets, Pine Martins and Polecats. Some of the modern Plummer terrier males are outstanding both in working ability and aesthetic appeal. Some of the bitches are shelly with tiny heads and a courage far exceeding their physical capabilities. To remedy these problems I introduced more bull terrier blood. The dog I chose was of dubious pedigree but a model of soundness, I mated her to a small Plummer Terrier dog, Curtis Price's Mask, a dog which had seen service with Foxhound packs.

Eight puppies were born from the union all brindle and white and all grew to roughly 14.5" at the shoulder. I kept back three puppies 'Seven' and 'Nine' now with Legion Kennels, Western Isles, Scotland, 'Lucy' with Lee Warren – two bitches and a dog – each were trained to a high standard. All hunted well and retrieved to hand for a distance of up to half a mile – and I confess to boost my own ego – I gave public exhibitions of the dogs working, retrieving and catching quarry.

THE PLUMMER TERRIER®
CLUB OF GREAT BRITAIN
BREED STANDARD

General Character

A Plummer Terrier should be strong, hardy, active and adaptable, with terrier characteristics and as much substance as possible. They should be equally at home in the house as in the kennel, be highly intelligent, courageous and tenacious. Affectionate, loyal and trustworthy with family and friends, yet should present a bright, alert appearance without displaying any excessive aggression or nervousness.

Head

Medium sized, full of quality with strong bones and powerful cheek and jaw muscles. Slight bull terrier characteristics are encouraged as is a well defined stop.

Ears

Dropped, rounded and neatly pinned to head. Prick or rose ears are not encouraged.

Eyes

Dark, prominent and oval, set widely apart.

Muzzle

Strong. Lips close with no excessive looseness. Teeth strong and even with full scissor bite. Nose black.

Neck

Strong, elegant, especially in the case of bitches, and

well carried.

Shoulders and forelegs
Strong, well laid back and developed without excessive muscle tone. Forelegs should be set square and straight and not tied in. Feet should be well shaped and dense. No resemblance of bend in front.

Back, hindquarters and hind legs
Back and loins, muscular, strong and well coupled, with well defined muscle development. Hindquarters should be lengthy and strong, with a well set on tail. Hindlegs – second thigh should be strong and muscular. Hocks clean and flat, turning neither inwards nor outwards. The hindleg must not be too bent. Feet well shaped and dense.

Body
Square in appearance when viewed from side i.e. distance of shoulder to ground. Depth through the heart should be easily spanned by two hands placed just behind the shoulders.

Tail
Carried high. Preferably docked and balanced to the size of the dog. Curled tails not encouraged.

Coat
Short, close and without guard hairs, yet with the ability to withstand weather. Loose / broken coats not acceptable.

Colour and markings

A bright fiery red tan with white. Full cape markings from head to tail, or a broad collar of white between head and shoulders are encouraged. Underside of the belly and chest, front and rear legs should be white although flecking is acceptable. Head either solid colour or with stripe or badger marked. Red self-coloured terriers, tri-coloured, brindle black or black and white terriers should not be encouraged.

Height

Maximum height to the shoulder, dog or bitch 14 inches.

Movement

Should be light, energetic, free, true and forcible and cover the ground. Hocks should be flexed under the body with straight powerful leverage.

Faults

Undershot or overshot mouths. Unsoundness, coarsness or displaying an hereditary fault.

Revised 2004

BREED FOUNDATION NOTES

Dominance and the Plummer Terrier

When the Austrian monk, Mendel experimented with his green peas he had the bad luck to happen upon the minor (but common and important) phenomenon that is today called 'dominance'. It confused him and biologists for many years. For one of his experiments he mated a tall pea with a dwarf, instead of this first generation being an 'intermediate' as one could logically have presumed, the following was produced:

- One tall pea that bred true
- One dwarf pea that bred true
- Two talls that repeated the parents performance

This result shows us that in the peas experimented with the tall gene was 'completely dominant' over the dwarf. Other instances of the dominant characteristic were also found, such as colouring (yellow over green) and smoothness (smooth over rough). A multitude of them have since been found in almost every kind of plant and animal, including Man (the 'Hapsburg lip', a slightly over grown lower jaw characterised in the Spanish and Austrian Royal families, is dominant to a 'normal' mouth).

Generally speaking useful normal characteristics are more common than defects because 'defective' individuals do not live long enough to breed, whilst healthy individuals do.

So we turn our attention to Plummer terriers and experiment by mating our true bred Plummer to a fell terrier (i.e. a Nuttall as has been done in the past). The first generation of pups would be black (black is dominant over the Plummer red and white – see Fig 1) and would be genetically termed an F1 with a label Fp (capital F for dominant and lower p for recessive).

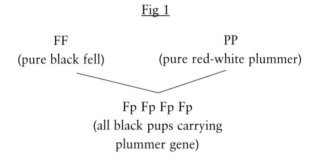

Fig 1

FF
(pure black fell)

PP
(pure red-white plummer)

Fp Fp Fp Fp
(all black pups carrying
plummer gene)

This litter of pups are taken back to another true Plummer to produce the F2 generation (Fig 2).

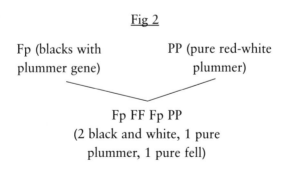

Fig 2

Fp (blacks with
plummer gene)

PP (pure red-white
plummer)

Fp FF Fp PP
(2 black and white, 1 pure
plummer, 1 pure fell)

The Plummer Bible

The PP pups are genetically pure breeding red and white terriers, the Fp pups black and white carrying no red genes (but could carry putty and tricolouring).

We now know that the red and white colouring of the typical Plummer terrier is 'recessive' to the black.

RECESSIVE FACTORS TRICOLOURING

Apart from the 'recessive red-white' there are other recessive factors in the phenotype i.e. the tricolour gene is recessive to red-white and therefore has managed to survive within the breed for a long time.

It can only be hoped that with a little careful breeding the tricolours (white, black and red head and body markings) will vanish within the next 10 years. In fact the appearance of such an animal will within 50 years cause as much interest as a merle puppy in a litter of harlequin Great Danes – and be equally unacceptable to the discerning breeder of Plummer terriers!!!!

At one time the breed was totally free of such tricolours but three factors introduced them into the breed.

1. The mating of Jennie to Laddie produced wonderful pups, including Vampire, Warlock and Beltane yet their sister was tricoloured, an outstanding animal which won many terrier shows. Tricolour of such high quality is not surprising, Laddie's sire, Scrap, was tricoloured

and seldom bested at shows or faulted as a hunt terrier. A stray tricolour gene in Jennie's pedigree resulted in the production of tricolours.

2. Alan Thomas's Hamish (tricolour blood) was introduced deliberately to widen the gene pool and to give the type greater substance. Hamish was a national champion and produced Rollo when mated with Omega. Rollo in turn produced Ainsley Newton's bitch, a tricolour who became the dam of Pollit's Damien.

3. Further tricolour blood came from Errol Forsyth's Pip (one of the best terriers of his day, a fine looker and a great worker). He produced Tony Metcalf's Todd and Velvet, two of the best small terriers in Britain. He carried the tricolour factor and produced quite a few tricolours from red bitches. David Hancock also bred four tricolour bitches by mating Pip to a pedigree unknown Russell bitch.

Now let us examine the genetic make up of the tricolour in relation to the acceptable red and white of the same breed. Firstly tricolour is 'recessive' to red and white (and the now almost extinct reflex terriers), therefore tricolours cannot carry 'red-white' genes but red and white terriers can carry the 'tricolour' genes (see Fig 1).

Fig 1

The result of mating two tricolour carriers

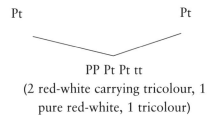

Pt   Pt

PP Pt Pt tt
(2 red-white carrying tricolour, 1
pure red-white, 1 tricolour)

Unless both sire and dam carry the tricolour factor no tricolour pups will be born. If only one parent carries the tricolour genes no tricolours will be born (see Fig 2).

Fig 2

The result of mating one tricolour carriers.

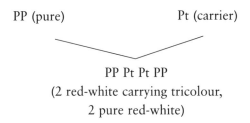

PP (pure)   Pt (carrier)

PP Pt Pt PP
(2 red-white carrying tricolour,
2 pure red-white)

Fig 3

The result of mating two tricolours

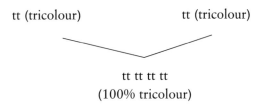

tt (tricolour)   tt (tricolour)

tt tt tt tt
(100% tricolour)

It is obvious therefore that mating a bitch known to carry tricolouring to a dog which has produced tricolours the result will be tricolours. However at least at present it would be wise not to avoid using a stud dog simply because it is a known carrier – the gene pool is too small to restrict it further would be unwise. Hopefully within a short period of time we shall see far less of this undesirable factor.

REFLEX TERRIERS

Reflex coloured terriers appeared as a result of fell terriers (i.e. Mr Nuttalls) being introduced to increase a very small gene pool. When mated to true red and white terriers the reflex coloured terriers will breed a fifty-fifty ratio of reflex to red-white pups.

The black and white terriers do not carry the red and white genes and likewise the red and white do not carry the black and white. If a reflex is mated the black and white are produced (see Fig 1).

Fig 1

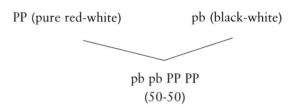

PP (pure red-white)   pb (black-white)

pb pb PP PP
(50-50)

Probably the best reflex stud dog used is the South Hereford Hunt terrier, Hector (from Rocky- pure Plummer and Raggy Dool – half bred, see Fig 2), this terrier has influenced the breed quite considerably but has not imported reflex genes into his red and white offspring.

Fig 2

Hectors Lineage

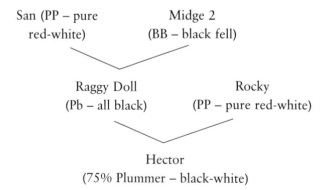

San (PP – pure   Midge 2
red-white)   (BB – black fell)

Raggy Doll   Rocky
(Pb – all black)   (PP – pure red-white)

Hector
(75% Plummer – black-white)

PROBLEMS OF INBREEDING WITH THE PLUMMER TERRIER

Taken from D B Plummer 'idiot sheets' 1990 and updated G Welsby 1993.

All sires and dams of any breed carry peculiarities, to minimise these problems and breed them out records are kept on each individual terrier used. Vampire's sire Laddie was the dog suspected of importing foul mouth.

Fig 1

Vampire – Laddie Lineage

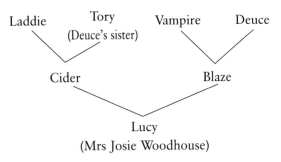

Lucy was mated to Vampire (whilst Brian was recovering from his heart attack) producing Magog and Gog. Magog was mated to Brian's other stud, Kotion producing Firebird (owner Mr C Price). For owners of Firebird bred bitches it is advisable to mate them with distant relatives of Vampire, at least four generations back to minimise the chance of foul mouth returning.

Laddie was bred at Chiddingford and Leconfield foxhound kennels by Derek Goddard (subsequently bought by Jim French, who liked Goddards dogs). Laddie produced Hulda from the bitch Deuce which had foul mouth (Brian gave her away and thought he had eliminated the problem). Granville Corn bred this line and unintentionally bred the peculiarity by accidentally bringing the lines together – it is still in the pedigree of Mayhem (Firebirds sister bred by Mrs D Dabnett) and the now dead Old Tom (Barry Johnson).

Cider also carried an untidy coat, this can be seen in her great granddaughter Firebird and her daughter Shona. Shona though like most of that line carries a good nose for scent (Brian relates the tale of how Cider would tackle otter and badger as fiercely as fox). Brian did not breed further from the carriers of the problems, i.e. Gog and Mayhem.

Warlock, Vampire and Beltane (produced from Laddie and Jennie) carried chocolate colouring and putty nose, so care is needed again not to breed their offspring too closely together. Beltane produced a chocolate pup but Omega did not. At the moment inbreeding is producing a fair number of this unwanted colouration, the only way to stop it is to not use the studs known to carry it. A register would help to locate and isolate problem areas.

PERTHE'S DISEASE

Fig 1

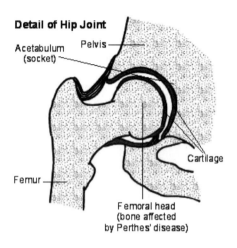

Detail of Hip Joint

Acetabulum (socket)

Pelvis

Cartilage

Femur

Femoral head (bone affected by Perthes' disease)

Perthe's Disease is an ailment that causes a deformed condition of the head of the femur and is associated with certain 3 – 8 year old children. However a very similar condition is associated with numerous young dogs, particularly terriers, and is only diagnosed accurately by x-ray examination of the animal.

Normally the head of the femur fits snugly into the acetabulum, a cup shaped cavity that allows the joint to articulate without causing the dog any pain. In Perthe's disease (and for dogs afflicted with a disorder called Oestochrondritis Dissecans, a disease in short legged terriers and Pekinese) the head of the femur becomes deformed and atrophied producing pain when the dog moves.

It is a fact that this disease also occurs in Plummer terriers but not in so great a frequency as other terrier types. However the PTA recognises this condition and does not try to hide it – other clubs are less than honest about the frequency of the disorder. This is unfortunate as by honesty alone can any congenital disorder can be eradicated (bred out) of a breed.

So common was this disorder amongst the mish mash of mongrel terrier types known as 'Jack Russells' that in 1976 when this terrier was Britain's most popular terrier that a society newspaper contributor wrote of "that cute little Jack Russell skip", totally unaware that the skip was caused by a rather painful physical disorder.

The disorder was first noticed here in the litter produced from mating Laddie and Jennie, producing Warlock, Vampire, Witch and Virdelack. Virdelack manifested the disorder to a lesser degree, it being diagnosed as either Oestochrondritis Dissecans or Perthe's Disease. Virdelack was given away, the owner agreeing not to breed of her, however the awareness was there that the disorder could occur in the breed at a later date.

'Blacks Veterinary Dictionary – 17th Edition' (edited by Geoffrey West) suggests that when the disease manifests itself the terrier might recover partially or completely. There is evidence to indicate that if the afflicted dog is denied exercise or only allowed very gentle exercise, the disease will usually clear up spontaneously within five or so months. Conversely an afflicted dog subjected to rigorous exercise will usually experience great pain and is unlikely to improve.

It is worrying to breed from any animal afflicted with Perthe's Disease, although there is some evidence to suggest an incorrectly balanced diet (P04/CA or vitamin C low) may induce or exacerbate the disorder. At the time of writing there is little scientifically tested evidence concerning the nature and cause of Perthe's Disease, but the malaise is almost certainly inherited.

PATELLA LUXATION
BY D B PLUMMER 1995

The patella, the knee cap, is a small fragment of bone that lies in front of what in animals is referred to as the stifle joint. When this bone is dislocated the disorder is known as Patella Luxation and the malaise is far from uncommon. Geoffrey West (1988) also mentions that Patella Luxation has been recorded in Boston Terriers, Boxers, Bulldogs, Cairn Terriers, Wire Fox Terriers, Griffons, Pekinese, Maltese, Papillions, Labradors, Scottish Terriers, King Charles Spaniels and it has been seen in West Highland White Terriers.

During the 1960s this disorder was very common amongst Jack Russell Terriers and at the Whaddon Chase Show in 1974 - 7 out of 22 exhibits displayed this disorder. No one admitted to breeding a terrier with a luxated patella yet one exhibit which was winning well in the 1970's had endured a surgical operation to correct this disorder.

Laddie is believed responsible for introducing the disorder into the bloodlines of the Plummer terrier. Warlock was suspected of suffering a slight case of patella luxation (unconfirmed by a vet), though no hunt judge ever mentioned that he manifested the disorder (most hunt committees assumed that the judges knew everything about terrier confirmation).

Later when line breeding Laddie to one of his daughter, Vanity two puppies were produced with quite serious patella luxation, after which the deliberate use of Laddie to inbreed was stopped although he features in all the pedigrees of the Plummer terriers.

The disorder is very rare in the breed today though it may well manifest itself if breeders insist on inbreeding to certain stud dogs. Refuse to use a stud dog that showed serious patella luxation no matter how good the confirmation of the terrier. Ted Adsett once described Warlock as the most perfect terrier – Warlock was far from perfect!!!

PUTTY NOSE
BY DB PLUMMER 1995

At the time of writing putty noses are a little too common amongst Plummer terriers. The putty nose (and pale eyes that usually accompany the peculiarity) is a cosmetic problem that in no way hinders the terriers hunting ability or indicates that the animal is in any way inferior to those with black points.

In fact for some reason the majority of putty nosed Plummer terriers are usually more stronger built than acceptable specimens! Most putty nosed terriers have pale lemon-tan coats and yellow or brown eyes and pale pink eyelids.

It is a sad fact that some of the original studs (before registration) carried this problem and so passed it on.

Rocky (bred by Carl Pollitt) was a regular producer of the problem, his son Viper (a Rocky / Alpha dog) however has only produced one terrier to date with the problem, and is nowhere near as rampant as his sire for producing the malaise.

The problem is believed to be inherited and was introduced in one place by the Bull Terrier blood used. This is a simple recessive gene, produced by:

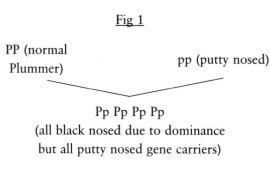

Fig 1

PP (normal Plummer)

pp (putty nosed)

Pp Pp Pp Pp
(all black nosed due to dominance but all putty nosed gene carriers)

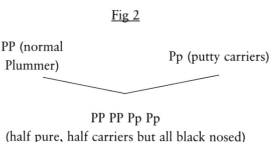

Fig 2

PP (normal Plummer)

Pp (putty carriers)

PP PP Pp Pp
(half pure, half carriers but all black nosed)

Fig 3

Pp (suspected carrier)   pp (putty nosed)

Pp pp Pp pp
(half putty nosed, half black nosed but carriers)

The only way to test a suspect is to use it on a phenotype that has the putty factor. In Fig 3 we can see that at best each dog born is a carrier. The only way to eradicate the problem is if such dogs are not bred from.

If normal coloured terriers carrying the putty nose factor are mated 25% of the pups will be putty, 50% black nosed carriers and 25% pure black nosed (see Fig 4).

Fig 4

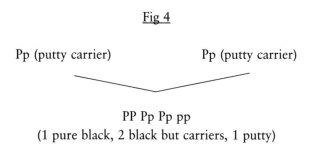

Pp (putty carrier)   Pp (putty carrier)

PP Pp Pp pp
(1 pure black, 2 black but carriers, 1 putty)

Clearly it is vitally important to be perfectly honest about which sires and dams carry the factor, and to mate carriers to non-carriers to eradicate this cosmetic problem.

It is obvious that the sire Tarka introduced the factor to the breed but it should also be made clear that some putty nosed Plummers have proven excellent and reliable workers to all quarry.

MR. I K FELCH'S LINE BREEDING SYSTEM

The union of parent and offspring is much less injurious than that of full siblings, the offspring having only half the blood of one parent, but this too must be kept within limits. Other relationships may also be carried far, providing that VARIETY be found between the blood of the two individuals mated. By bearing this principle in mind a strain may be successfully established from two individuals alone and carried on for many years without a cross.

Mr. Felch, a veteran judge and breeder of fowl in America, many years ago published a book (called Poultry Culture), a chart showing at a glance the main principle on which line breeding should be done. The chart has been of practical benefit to breeders and has been improved and reproduced with modifications to make its meaning more clear.

The strain originates from two individuals only, they were perfectly vigorous and healthy and either UNRELATED or only distantly related by blood (difficult for the Plummer terrier breeding at the time of writing).

They should be from two different kennels, it is found that even the change of ground has some effect on producing 'different blood' which helps avoid congenital diseases.

Taking two original units (dog and bitch) Mr Felch's chart shows how they may be bred to maintain health and vigour.

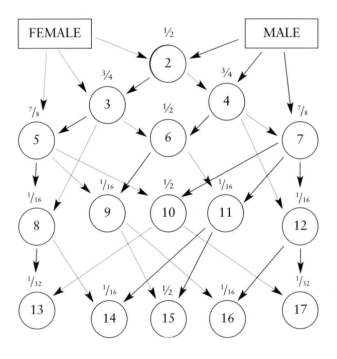

The Plummer Bible

The dotted lines denote bitches, the solid lines males. Two lines meet at a point, the circle denotes that point and the produce of the mating, the number distinguishes the produce or group. The fraction outside the circle denotes the mixture or proportion in that product of original blood from which the strain is bred.

In the first year for example , the first pair produce group 2, whose blood is half and half of each. The second year the original bitch (or if needed litter sister) is bred to a dog from group 2 and the original dog bred to a bitch from group 2. These unions produce group 3 and 4, each of which possesses three quarters of the blood from the original parent on its own side of the chart. The mates taken from group 2 must be carefully selected to type, according to that "course of selection".

The third year a dog from group 3 is mated to the original bitch to produce group 5 and a bitch from group 4 to original dog to produce group 7. All these possess seven-eighths of the blood on their own side of the original parents and are to be rigourously selected TRUE TO TYPE as before.

The most noteworthy mating of the third year is a bitch from group 3 with a dog of group 4 producing group 6. All members of group 6 possess equal (or half-half) blood from the original parents, like those from group 2. A bitch from group 5 and dog from group 7 will again produce half-half blood in group

10. Matings of full brothers and sisters to produce similar equality of blood (i.e. incestuous in-breeding) would have resulted in swift degeneracy. As it is the matings are made from lines that are mainly characterised by the original pair and yet preserved the mathematically exact equality of blood in group 10.

A generation further on group 15 is produced from groups 9 and 11 or groups 8 and 12, or the produce of the former may be mated to the latter. It is possible to see that half-half blood of a cross can be kept intact and exact, without any loss of size, fertility or vigour. It is also seen that by the time you get to group 10 there are virtually 3 strains – half-half, thirteen-sixteenths of the bitch bloodline (group 8) and thirteen-sixteenths of the male bloodline (group 12). Yet all are related sufficiently to prevent evil and all have gone through the same "course of selection" towards the fixed TYPE.

Whenever a cross is necessary in a strain the chart also shows the procedure that should be followed. The cross is treated as a new unit and the produce re-mated back to the 'homestrain' in the same way as before. Breeders call this 'breeding back to a strain' and the philosophy of it can be clearly understood from the chart as previous page.

However difficulties can be encountered, it should be remembered that Mr. Felch was only dealing with fowl, problems that might arise in the formation of the infant fowl are eradicated in the egg – therefore inherited defects were not as common as the stricken pullets never hatch!!

The Plummer Bible